Creatures of the De...

SPECTACULAR SQUID

Casey Rand

www.raintreepublishers.co.uk
Visit our website to find out more information about Raintree books.

To order:
- Phone 0845 6044371
- Fax +44 (0) 1865 312263
- Email myorders@raintreepublishers.co.uk

Customers from outside the UK please telephone +44 1865 312262

Raintree is an imprint of Capstone Global Library Limited, a company incorporated in England and Wales having its registered office at 7 Pilgrim Street, London, EC4V 6LB – Registered company number: 6695582

Text © Capstone Global Library Limited 2011
First published in hardback in 2011
Paperback edition first published in 2012
The moral rights of the proprietor have been asserted.

All rights reserved. No part of this publication may be reproduced in any form or by any means (including photocopying or storing it in any medium by electronic means and whether or not transiently or incidentally to some other use of this publication) without the written permission of the copyright owner, except in accordance with the provisions of the Copyright, Designs and Patents Act 1988 or under the terms of a licence issued by the Copyright Licensing Agency, Saffron House, 6–10 Kirby Street, London EC1N 8TS (www.cla.co.uk). Applications for the copyright owner's written permission should be addressed to the publisher.

Edited by Megan Cotugno and Abby Colich
Designed by Philippa Jenkins
Picture research by Hannah Taylor
Originated by Capstone Global Library Ltd
Printed and bound in China by CTPS

ISBN 978 1 406 22636 2 (hardback)
15 14 13 12 11
10 9 8 7 6 5 4 3 2 1

ISBN 978 1 406 22643 0 (paperback)
16 15 14 13 12
10 9 8 7 6 5 4 3 2 1

British Library Cataloguing in Publication Data
Rand, Casey.
Spectacular squid. -- (Creatures of the deep)
1. Squids--Juvenile literature. 2. Deep-sea animals--Juvenile literature.
I. Title II. Series
594.5'8-dc22
A full catalogue record for this book is available from the British Library.

Acknowledgements
We would like to thank the following for permission to reproduce photographs:

© Kevin Raskoff p. **20**; © Seapics.com p. **14** (David Shen); Alamy Images p. **13** (© WaterFrame); Corbis pp. **17** (© Visuals Unlimited), **29** (© EPA/Christopher Berkey); FLPA pp. **9**, **11** (Minden Pictures/Norbert Wu), **10** (D P Wilson), **18** (Minden Pictures/Fred Bavendam); Image courtesy of the Monterey Bay Aquarium Research Institute p. **23**; Image Quest Marine p. **5**; naturepl.com pp. **6**, **15** (David Shale); Photolibrary pp. **4** (OSF/Mark Deeble & Victoria Stone), **21** (OSF/Mark Conlin), **27** bottom (Pacific Stock/James Watt); Rex Features p. **24** (Newspix); Science Photo Library pp. **16** (Dante Fenolio), **22** (Alexis Rosenfeld); SeaPics.com pp. **12** (Bob Cranston), **19** (Mark Strickland); Shutterstock p. **27** top (© erwinova).

Cover photograph of Glass squid reproduced with permission of © Image Quest Marine.

We would like to thank Michael Bright for his invaluable help in the preparation of this book.

Every effort has been made to contact copyright holders of material reproduced in this book. Any omissions will be rectified in subsequent printings if notice is given to the publisher.

Disclaimer
All the Internet addresses (URLs) given in this book were valid at the time of going to press. However, due to the dynamic nature of the Internet, some addresses may have changed, or sites may have changed or ceased to exist since publication. While the author and publisher regret any inconvenience this may cause readers, no responsibility for any such changes can be accepted by either the author or the publisher.

CONTENTS

The mysterious deep sea 4
The glass squid 6
Squid parts 8
The squid life 10
Flying squid 12
The hunters and the hunted 14
Disappearing act 16
Camouflage squid 18
Exploring the deep sea 20
Alien squid 22
Monsters of the sea 24
Man vs squid 26
Squid in danger 28
Glossary 30
Find out more 31
Index 32

Some words are printed in bold, **like this**. You can find out what they mean by looking in the glossary.

THE MYSTERIOUS DEEP SEA

Far below the surface of the ocean lies an entire world of unknown and mysterious animals and **organisms**. Many of these creatures have never been seen or studied by humans. In many ways, scientists know more about outer space than they do about what goes on deep in our own sea. The deep sea is Earth's final frontier, still waiting to be fully explored with many mysteries to be revealed.

Exploring the ocean

Deep in the ocean there are enormous amounts of **pressure**, small amounts of light, and very cold temperatures. To explore these cold, dark, high-pressure areas, scientists must use special **chambers** made of steel, or other strong materials, to protect themselves.

Special vehicles are used to explore the deep sea.

Scientists estimate there are more than nine million **species** of animals yet to be discovered in the ocean.

Squid family

One of the most exciting animals that lives in the deep sea is the squid. There are over 300 amazing species, or types, of squid already discovered in the ocean. There are likely to be many more undiscovered species.

THE GLASS SQUID

The glass squid family includes more than 60 different **species** of squid. They have this name because, like glass, most of them are almost completely **transparent**! This helps them avoid **predators**, or animals that might want to eat them.

Creatures great and small

Glass squid range in size from very tiny to enormous. The piglet squid is only 100 millimetres (4 inches) long, while the colossal squid may reach 15 metres (almost 50 feet)! Despite their differences, they are both members of the glass squid family and are closely related.

The piglet squid is one of the smallest known glass squid.

100 millimetres (4 inches)

Ocean zones

Scientists divide the ocean into five zones. These zones include the water's surface and the ocean floor. Glass squid can be found from the sunlight zone down to the cold, dark abyssal zone.

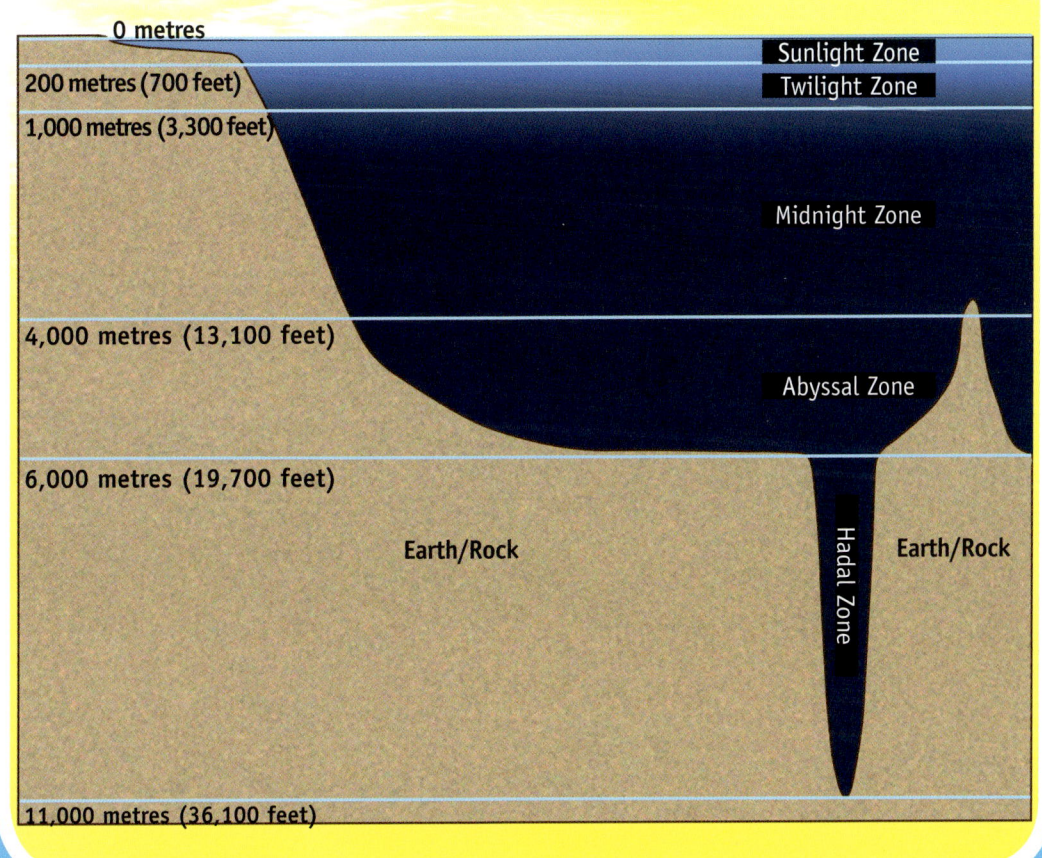

Home of the glass squid

Glass squid live in saltwater throughout the world's oceans. Some glass squid stay deep below the ocean's surface, but others live near the surface.

SQUID PARTS

Did you know that squid have three hearts? Squid have two small hearts for pumping blood to their **gills**, the structures through which they breathe. They also have one larger heart for pumping blood to the rest of their body.

Squid brains

Squid are some of the most intelligent **invertebrates**, or animals without backbones. Squid have a large head made of **cartilage**, like the material in your ears, which holds a large brain.

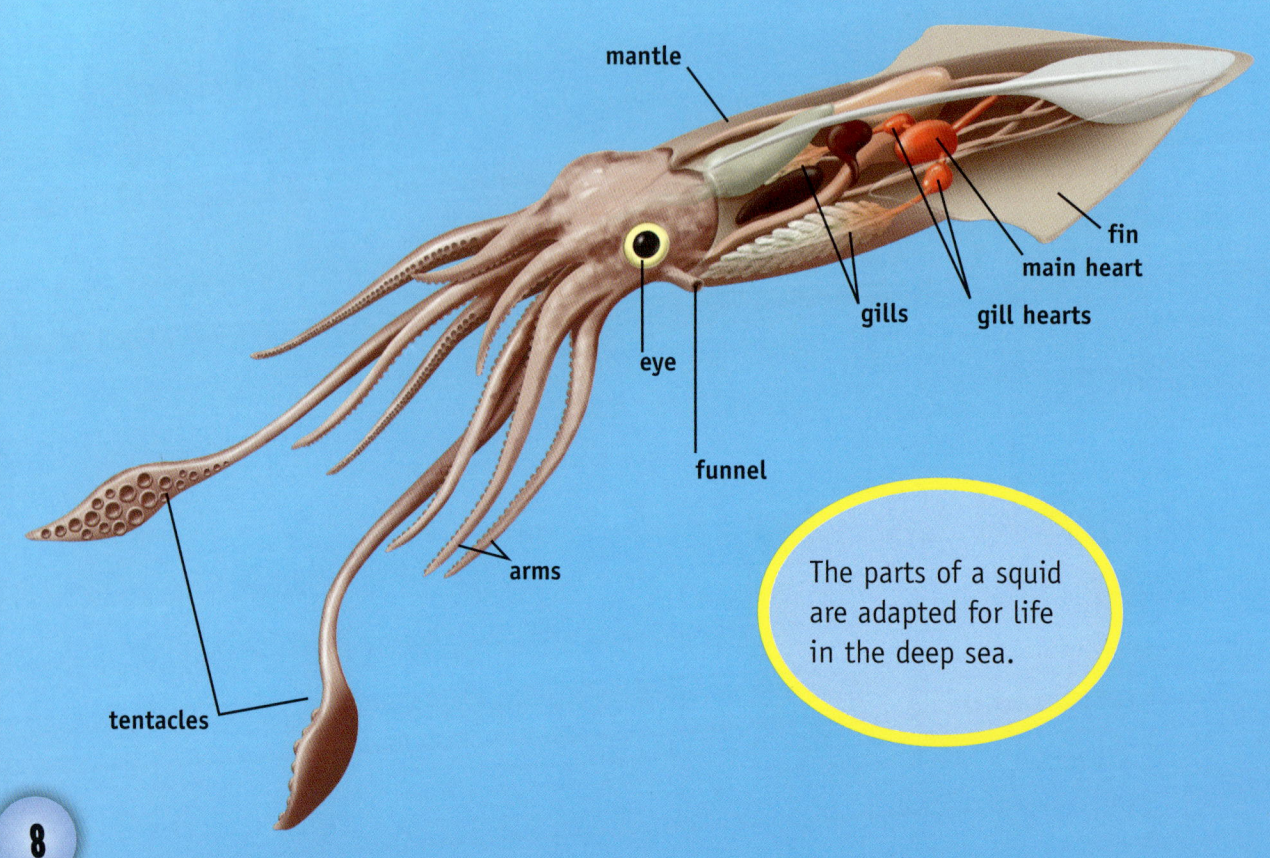

The parts of a squid are adapted for life in the deep sea.

Squid vs octopus

The squid and octopus families are similar, but not the same.

Characteristic	Squid	Octopus
Size	more than 20 metres (66 feet)	less than 5 metres (16 feet)
Arms	8 arms and 2 tentacles	8 arms
Suckers	suction cups with hooks (usually)	suction cups
Fins	2 fins	none (usually)

This eight-armed octopus swims under water.

Fit for sea

The body of the squid is built to survive the deep sea. The squid does not have bones. Bones could be crushed by the enormous **pressure** of the deep sea. Squid muscles contain a liquid called **ammonia**. Ammonia is lighter than water. This helps the squid move easily through the water.

THE SQUID LIFE

An average squid lives anywhere from one to two years. They usually live in the same area for most of their lives. However, they usually **migrate** before **reproducing**.

Squid love

There are male and female squid, and squid reproduction is **sexual**. Many types of squid travel alone, but during mating season they swarm together into large groups. Female squid can carry as many as 10 million eggs. Once the eggs are **fertilized**, the female will attach them to a rock or leave them in a safe area. Squid die after they reproduce.

Adult squid swarm together during mating season.

Squid eggs are placed in a safe place and left to grow alone.

Baby squid

When baby squid hatch from their eggs, they may appear to be tiny versions of adult squid. Since adult squid die after reproducing, baby squid must survive on their own. These mini squid stay near the surface of the water where they feed on **plankton** and grow stronger. As they grow, squid move further and further below the surface of the water.

FLYING SQUID

Squid are the fastest moving **invertebrates** in the ocean. The Humboldt squid is known as the jumbo flying squid. It can swim at 25 kilometres (16 miles) per hour! It sometimes swims so fast to avoid **predators** that it throws itself out of the water – flying a short distance in the air.

This Humboldt squid was found in the waters surrounding Mexico.

Underwater jet propulsion

Squid have a unique way of swimming. A squid sucks water into a muscular **cavity** called a **mantle** cavity. The squid then rapidly **contracts** the cavity, shooting the water out through a funnel. This propels, or moves, its body through the water. The squid's funnel can be aimed in any direction, so the squid can swim any way it chooses.

Pack attack

The Humboldt squid can grow to over 1.8 metres (6 feet) long and weigh up to 45 kilograms (100 pounds). Like all squid, they are carnivores, or meat-eaters. Humboldt squid hunt in schools of up to 1,200. They are very aggressive and will even eat each other if other food is difficult to find.

This Humboldt squid is eating a member of the same **species**!

THE HUNTERS AND THE HUNTED

Squid hunt many other animals for food, but they are also hunted by many animals. Fortunately for squid, they are talented hunters. They are also talented at escaping other **predators**.

Hunters

Squid are carnivores that hunt fish, shrimp, crabs, other squid, and many other underwater animals. Many squid hunt by staying very still and waiting for food to get close enough to grab.

The goblin shark is a predator of squid.

Squid have a bird-like beak used for tearing into their prey.

Beak

Tools of the hunt

Most squid have two long tentacles. The ends are covered in suction cups and hooks. These are used for grabbing **prey**. These tentacles also have sensors that tell the squid whether the prey will taste nice or not. The tentacles pass captured food to the squid's eight arms, which pull the prey in to be eaten.

Hunted

Squid are hunted by many deep-sea creatures such as goblin sharks, whales, and eels. Even the biggest squid, those nearly 15 metres (49 feet) long, are eaten by the sperm whale, which may grow up to 19 metres (62 feet) long.

DISAPPEARING ACT

Squid have amazing talents for escaping **predators**. Many glass squid are clear. This makes them very difficult to see. Some other types of squid can nearly disappear to avoid predators!

Squid lights

Certain squid, such as the firefly squid, have **photophores**. Photophores are special cells that can produce light, just like a torch. Squid can use this light to make their shadow disappear. Or the squid can use a flash of bright light to temporarily blind a predator, giving the squid time to escape.

The firefly squid can make its own light.

Can squid ink cure diseases?

Recently, scientists have found that squid ink is toxic to certain types of cancer cells. There is more research to do, but squid ink may help cure diseases one day.

Ink cannon

Most squid produce and store a dark ink. A squid can shoot this ink into the water and disappear before predators realize what has happened.

Squid ink contains **melanin**, the same substance that gives your skin its colour.

CAMOUFLAGE SQUID

The Caribbean Reef Squid can change colour to blend in with almost any environment. This is known as camouflage, but unlike camouflage trousers, these squid can quickly change colour! Camouflage helps the Reef Squid hide from **predators** and sneak up on **prey**.

Coat of many colours

Chromatophores are cells in the skin of the Reef Squid. Each chromatophore has a certain colour. These are similar to the cells that make your eyes look blue, green, hazel, or brown. But the squid has many different coloured chromatophores. This allows the squid to rapidly change from green to blue.

Reef Squid can change colour and pattern to disappear into the background.

Reef Squid can use each side of their body to send a different message at the same time!

Colour communication

Squid can use colour changes to communicate with each other. They send messages to other squid by changing colour, showing patterns of colour, and by flashing certain colours. In fact, some squid can send two different messages to different squid at the same time.

EXPLORING THE DEEP SEA

There are thousands of deep-sea animals that scientists know very little about, and thousands of others that remain undiscovered. To learn about these creatures, scientists have to find a way to explore the deepest parts of the ocean.

This rarely photographed deep-sea creature is a type of octopus.

The Aquarius Reef Base allows scientists to study the underwater world.

Danger in the deep sea

The deep sea is filled with danger. The water in the deep sea has very little oxygen and very low temperatures. Even more dangerous are the high **pressure** levels found there. Water presses down on everything below it. Deep in the sea, there is a lot of water pushing down from above, creating high pressure. This makes exploring the deep sea very difficult.

Astronauts of the sea

To study the deep sea, scientists use special equipment that can handle the pressure and cold temperatures. Some scientists work in a special underwater laboratory to study sea life. The scientists who work there are known as **aquanauts**. They can stay underwater for weeks at a time in the laboratory.

ALIEN SQUID

The development of sea laboratories and **submersibles** (small vehicles built to explore underwater) has led to the discovery of many mysterious sea creatures. Some of the most amazing are a group of large, interesting squid that scientists are now beginning to learn about.

Alien encounter

In 1988 the crew of a manned submersible called *Nautile* made a remarkable discovery. At over 4,500 metres (15,000 feet) deep they spotted a huge squid with very long arms. The squid was unlike any that anyone had ever seen. This squid has since been named the long-armed squid.

Nautile is a manned submersible used to search the deep sea.

This mysterious squid with arms 10 metres (33 feet) long was seen lurking in the Gulf of Mexico.

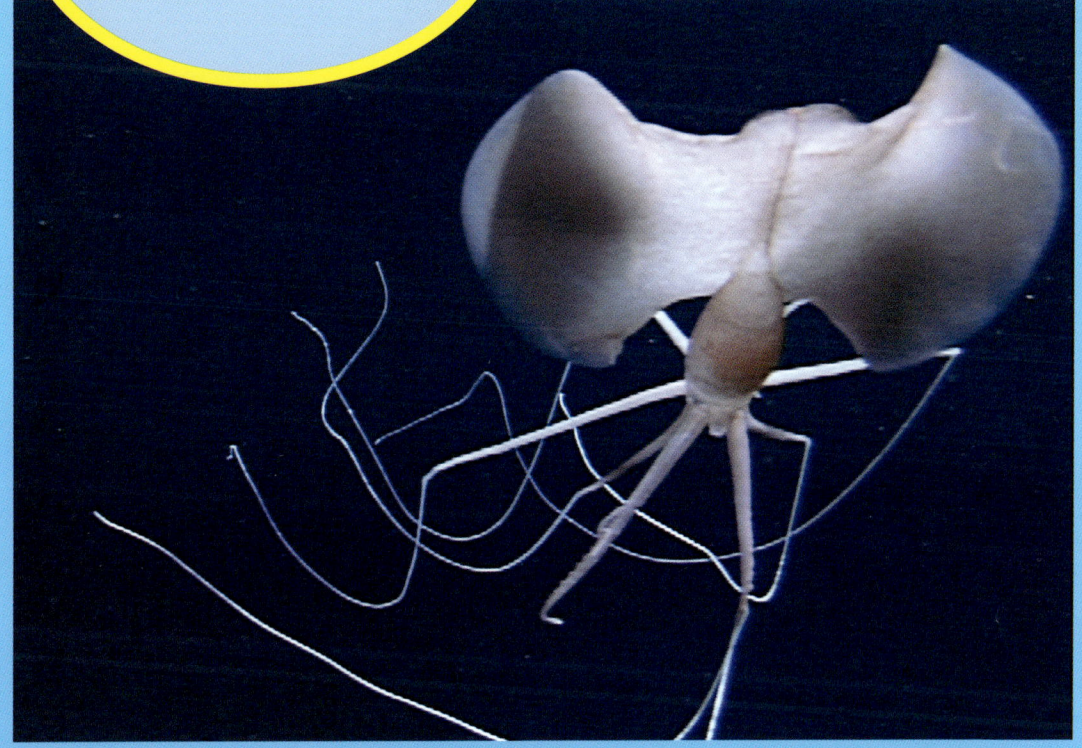

Long-armed squid

Since the first sighting of the long-armed squid, several of these squid have been spotted by submersibles. However, scientists have not been able to capture and study any adult long-armed squid. We know that these squid have large fins, large eyes, and extremely long arms. Otherwise, these squid remain mysterious – almost completely unknown to humans.

MONSTERS OF THE SEA

Deep below the surface of the sea live monstrous squid even larger than the long-armed squid. These squid stay hidden in the deepest, darkest parts of the ocean. We know very little about them.

Giant squid

The first discovery of a giant squid occurred 900 metres (2,950 feet) deep in the ocean. The largest giant squid ever found was 18 metres (59 feet) long. They have eyes as large as footballs! The giant squid is only the second largest of the squid. Scientists have discovered another even larger squid, named the colossal squid. It is the largest known **invertebrate** on Earth.

This 227 kilogram (500 pound) giant squid was found dead off the coast of Australia.

Giant killer

While these giant squid are near the top of the **food chain**, they are hunted by an even bigger animal – the massive sperm whale. The beaks of giant squid are often found in the bellies of sperm whales. Some whales even have scars from doing battle with giant squid.

Squid Sizes

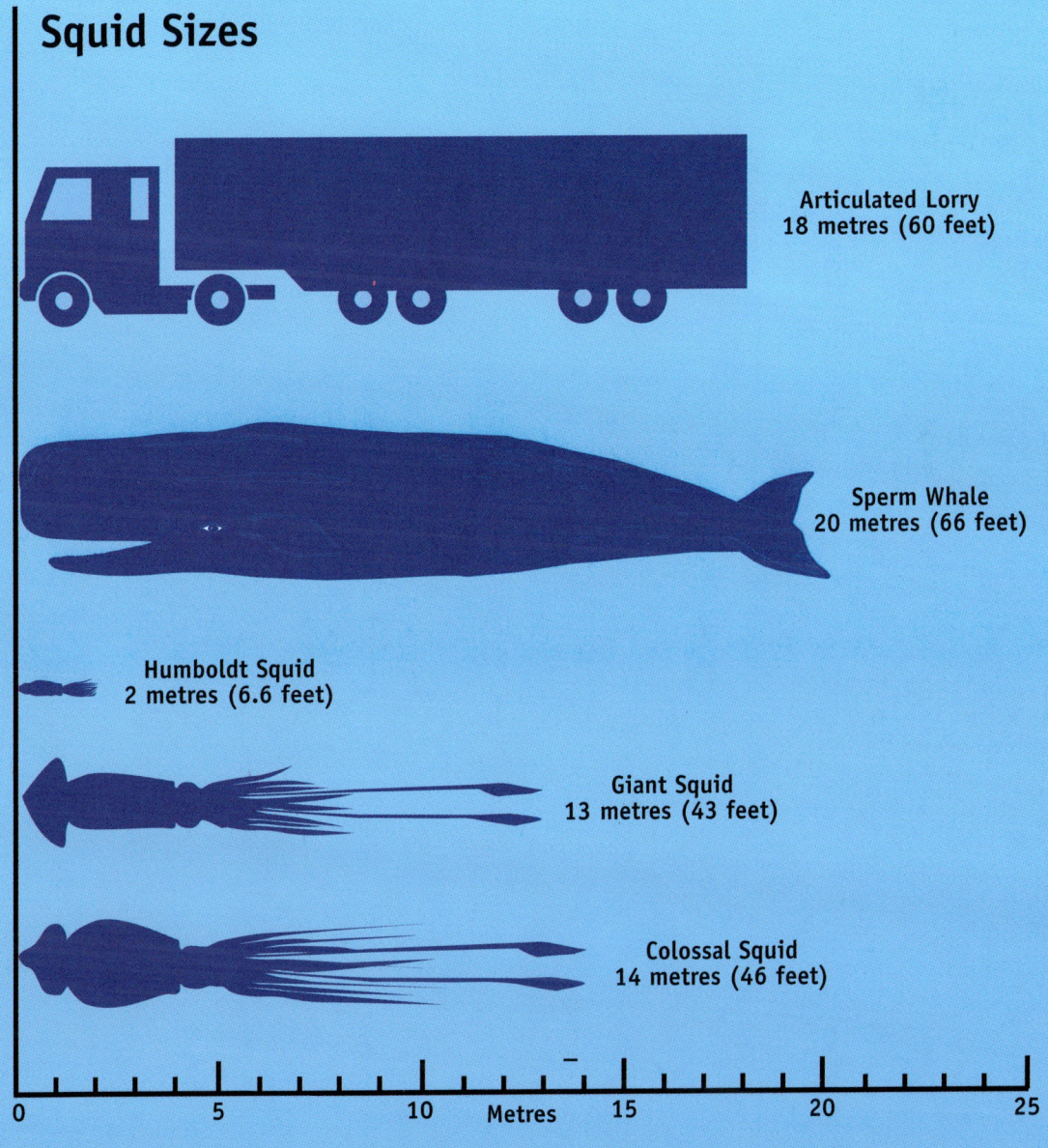

Articulated Lorry
18 metres (60 feet)

Sperm Whale
20 metres (66 feet)

Humboldt Squid
2 metres (6.6 feet)

Giant Squid
13 metres (43 feet)

Colossal Squid
14 metres (46 feet)

MAN VS SQUID

Squid are known to be aggressive and skilled hunters. But do squid ever attack humans or ships?

Tales from the sea

For centuries sailors have told stories of giant creatures in the dark waters of the sea. After World War II, survivors of some sunken ships told stories of men being pulled from ships and eaten by giant squid-like monsters. But none of these stories have been officially verified. It is still a mystery whether giant squid could really attack a ship.

Fishing for squid

Fisheries are businesses that rear or catch underwater animals to sell, usually for food. While some squid are eaten by humans, most deep-sea squid are not. These squid have packets of **ammonia** that make them taste very bad to humans. However, deep-sea squid hunt some of the same fish that fisheries catch. This may make it more difficult for these squid to find enough food.

SQUID IN DANGER

While deep-sea squid are not fished by humans for food, the activities of humans can affect all life in the oceans, including deep-sea squid.

Harmful emissions

Scientists believe **CO_2 emissions** are causing a decrease in oxygen levels in ocean water. This may cause some squid, such as the Humboldt squid, to become less active, and therefore more likely to be eaten by **predators**. This could significantly affect the **food chain** and is a major concern for scientists.

Spilled oil

In 2010, an oil well in the Gulf of Mexico was damaged and began spilling oil into the sea. Oil is known to be poisonous to almost all life-forms. While deep-sea squid may not come into direct contact with this oil, **plumes** of oil deep underwater may harm them. And many of the fish, shrimp, and other animals that squid hunt are harmed by oil spills. This could cause a dangerous shortage of food for deep-sea squid.

Floating oil can be extremely dangerous to sea life.

GLOSSARY

ammonia colourless, smelly substance that is lighter than water

aquanauts name for scientists who work in laboratories in the ocean

cartilage elastic-like connective tissue found in various parts of the body, such as the joints

cavity unfilled space in a mass, such as a rock

chamber room

chromatophore cell that contains a coloured pigment and can, by expansion or contraction, change the colour of the skin

CO_2 emissions carbon dioxide gas that has been released into the air

contract squeeze or force together

fertilize begin reproduction

fishery place where fish or other aquatic animals are caught to be sold

food chain chain of animals and organisms in a region that rely on each other for food

gill organ through which a fish or underwater animal breathes

invertebrate animal without a backbone

mantle main body of the squid that holds the brain, lungs, heart, and other organs

melanin substance that gives skin its colour

migrate move from one place to another

organism living thing

photophore light-producing organ found especially in underwater animals

plankton collection of small or microscopic organisms that float or drift in fresh or saltwater, especially at or near the surface

plume column or band of a substance

predator animal that hunts other animals

pressure weight or force that pushes against something

prey animal hunted or caught for food

reproduce to have babies

sexual type of reproduction in which organisms mate

species group of animals and plants that are similar and can reproduce

submersible small underwater craft

transparent something that is clear or can be seen through

FIND OUT MORE

Books

Octopuses and Squid (Scary Creatures), Gerald Legg (Book House, 2004)

Deep Sea, Richard Spilsbury (A & C Black, 2009)

Ocean Food Chains (Protecting Food Chains), Heidi Moore (Raintree, 2010)

Websites

ngkids.co.uk/inside_scoop/1444/steve_backshall_s_extreme_animal_files_6
Find out about the tiny but deadly blue ringed octopus which changes its colour when threatened.

www.bbc.co.uk/learningzone/clips/the-behaviour-of-deep-sea-squid-and-octopus/10504.html
Watch this amazing video about how bioluminescence is used to distract predators.

www.visitsealife.com/London/explore-our-creatures/octopus.aspx
Did you know that octopuses have three hearts and blue blood? Find out more fun octopus facts on this website.

INDEX

ammonia 9, 26
aquanauts 21
arms 9, 15, 22, 23

babies 11
beaks 15, 25
bodies 8, 9
bones 8, 9
brains 8

camouflage 18
Caribbean Reef Squid 18
carnivores 13, 14
cartilage 8
chromatophores 18
CO_2 emissions 28
colour 18, 19
colossal squid 6, 24, 25
communication 19

depth 4, 7, 9, 11, 20, 21, 22, 24
diseases 17

eggs 10, 11
escape 12, 16, 17
exploration 4, 20, 21, 22, 23
eyes 18, 23, 24

females 10
fins 9, 23
firefly squid 16
fisheries 26
food chain 25, 28

giant squid 24, 25, 26
gills 8
glass squid 6, 7, 16
Gulf of Mexico 28

heads 8
hearts 8
hooks 9, 15
Humboldt squid 12, 13, 25, 28
hunting 13, 14, 15, 26, 28

ink 17
intelligence 8
invertebrates 8, 12, 24

laboratories 21, 22
long-armed squid 22, 23

males 10
mantle cavity 13
mating season 10
migration 10

Nautile (submersible) 22

octopuses 9, 20
oil spills 28
oxygen 21, 28

photophores 16
piglet squid 6
plankton 11
plumes 28

predators 6, 12, 14, 16, 17, 18, 25, 26, 28
pressure 4, 9, 21
prey 11, 13, 14, 15, 18, 26, 28

reproduction 10, 11

saltwater 7
scientists 4, 7, 17, 20, 21, 22, 23, 24, 28
sizes 6, 9, 13, 15, 24, 25
species 5, 6
sperm whales 15, 25
submersibles 22, 23
suckers 9
suction cups 9, 15
sunlight 4
swimming 9, 12, 13

temperatures 4, 21
tentacles 9, 15

zones 7

32